The Six Most Powerful Sales Questions ...

and how they can increase your income

Lawrence Leyton

Editor: Lisa Minsky

Jacket design: Jane Davidson

First published in Great Britain in 2002 by LLI, London

Copyright © 2002 LLI

All rights reserved. No part of this publication
may be reproduced, stored in a retrieval system,
or transmitted in any form or by any means,
electronic, mechanical, photocopying, recording or
otherwise, without prior written permission of the
copyright owner.

A CIP catalogue record for this book is available
from the British Library

ISBN 0-9543242-0-X

Manufactured in the UK by Antony Rowe Ltd,
Chippenham, Wiltshire

The mind is like a parachute, it works best when it is opened!

ABOUT THE AUTHOR

Lawrence Leyton is a high-level international speaker, broadcaster and an expert in the field of human behaviour and peak performance. He has consulted for many of the world's top companies, including Microsoft, Lucent, Ford, MRI, AstraZeneca, Prudential and Aventis.

His expertise is in the fields of innovation and communication, and his research into human performance has been featured on many television shows, both in the UK and abroad. Lawrence has had his own television special, which was shown on ITV at peak time, gaining an audience of 8.6 million. He is currently working on his second series.

Lawrence is also a clinical hypnotherapist, specialising in helping people overcome phobias and addictions. He has coached many world-class athletes in their preparation for the Olympic Games in order to help them achieve peak mental performance. Lawrence is a highly skilled neuro-linguistic practitioner and thought field therapist.

"As someone who has attended several Anthony Robbins seminars, it was great to see a British motivator and coach of equal standing."

Paul Rayson, De Vere Hotels

"Without doubt you provided one of the high points of our conference and you can take much credit for its overall success for which you can never be thanked enough."

Jerome Adam OBE, Executive Director of Moores Roland International Europe

"The reaction from our marketing team has been simply excellent and they felt that it was an interactive learning experience. The messages that you gave the delegates have certainly been remembered and the techniques that you shared with all of us will definitely be implemented."

David Lock, Aventis Pharmaceuticals

"Just a very quick note to say that I was very impressed with your presentation on Friday last. I found your programme revealing and exciting, and it makes me wish I was 40 years younger.

I have been privileged to watch and listen to Tony Buzan and more locally Jack Black, but your presentation tops the lot. Keep up the good work, the business world needs you."

John Corcoran, Special Projects Co-ordinator, University of Glasgow

CONTENTS

Introduction

Unconscious buying

Question one – Towards v Away people

Question two – Sameness v Difference people

Question three – Detail v Overview people

Question four – Convincer Channels

Question five – Convincer Cycle

Question six – Procedure v Options people

Summary

Answers

The six questions

The six filters

Notes

"Sale" comes from the Swedish word *Selle* which means "to serve"

The more you sell, the more you serve!

INTRODUCTION

Thank you for buying this book. I hope you will find it of great value.

This book is not just for the professional salesperson. This book I believe will be useful to you no matter what profession you are in. It does not matter whether you are self-employed, a student or a professional, since I firmly believe that life is about selling.

By the way, I am not a professional salesman. "Oh my God", I hear you crying! "So what can he teach us?" Hang in there and hear me out...

All the way through my working career I have had to sell even though I didn't realise it at the time. It did not seem to matter what I was doing or how good an idea was, where the project fell down was when I had to convince someone to buy it.

If you think even from a very early age you are selling, for example trying to persuade your parents to buy you a dog or a new bike or that new dress or pair of expensive trainers.

When you are a student and go for an interview to get into university, you are selling. When you have left university and are trying to get a job, you are selling. When you are trying to convince your boss to give you a raise, you are selling. You could be the best actor or singer in the world but if you can't sell yourself during the audition, then the less competent actor will get the part over you. When you are trying to present an idea during a presentation to work colleagues or, worse, potential clients, you are selling.

Guess what – you are always selling!

You see, you don't have to be a pro and earn your living from selling to get the most out of this book.

I realised that in life you are always selling, whether it be selling products, services or just simply selling yourself. However the first thing that I would like to stress to any professionals reading this book is that I am not here to tell you how to suck eggs, how to sell. If you are reading this book, you are most probably an experienced salesperson and already have the basic skills of selling. You already know about the sales process and sales cycle, and if I was to try to include this in the book, then I am sure within a couple of minutes you would lose the will to live!

Instead of teaching you how to sell, I am going to take a different angle, since my expertise is in human behaviour. This includes how people behave when they buy a product. Natural-born salespeople instinctively use these techniques, but at an unconscious level since they don't normally have a conscious awareness of them. This is what we call "tacit knowledge".

I feel I have had enough knocks in life and enough projects break down on me to know how it feels to be rejected. Sometimes, because I could not sell myself, my ideas went down like a pork chop at a Jewish wedding! I soon realised that some people were gifted and were naturals in the art of selling. I desperately wanted to find out what it was that made them so good. *Bastards!* I wanted what they had.

I joked that some of the people that I knew were marketing beasts! They were so successful at selling themselves even though they did not have much to offer. Some of their stuff was pretty lame compared to what I felt I had to offer. But still, to be fair to the beasts, they had the competitive advantage.

But what was the secret of their success? When I started to tour the world speaking professionally, I had the good fortune to mix and mingle with lots of salesforces. Now at this point I was not speaking to them on sales, just on human potential and peak performance. But I got the opportunity to hear from the horse's mouth, so to speak – well, in fact, not actually the horse's mouth, but the horse's behaviour.

What was interesting was that I did not hear it directly from them, but instead I picked it up from watching them in action. The strangest thing was after hundreds of conversations with them, even they could not explain in words what made them so good at their job. They could not even attempt to write a book of techniques or a users' guide as in their mind they just did what they did.

"Explicit knowledge" is the sort of knowledge that you can pass on, as you have a total awareness of it. "Tacit knowledge" is the sort of knowledge that you have no awareness of and therefore you are unable to pass it on. For example, I could pass on to you how to stand on stage and how to project your voice in the correct way. I could pass on a technique, I could write it down in a book. But what I could not tell you is how to turn an audience around when they become difficult. How do you turn an audience from a harsh one to an audience eating out of the palm of your hand? It is just stuff I can do – well, not all the time! This is knowledge I could not write about or put into words. This is "tacit knowledge".

So by modelling the behaviour patterns of these super-salespeople and then understanding the unconscious patterns that their clients were using and the different variations, I began to find out the secrets to their success.

I also exhaustively studied other areas of alternative psychology, including neuro-linguistic programming, thought field therapy and clinical hypnosis. As a hypnotherapist, I have sat one on one with literally thousands of people who are in a trance state learning about the many different patterns of unconscious behaviour. On all of these and my own studies I base this book.

UNCONSCIOUS BUYING

I have studied extensively the many different unconscious patterns that people go through when they buy products and the patterns that all super-salespeople habitually use. Now I want to share with you those secrets so that you too can become a super-salesperson.

The first step is to have a greater awareness of people's unconscious buying patterns. You have to learn what to notice as people always reveal the information if you ask for it in the right way.

You will learn how to extract the information that you need by asking six simple questions.

The last step is to understand how to use that information to directly influence the sell. By the way, it does not matter what you are selling, from products or services, double-glazing and air-conditioning units to marketing services and consultancies.

At first these techniques or concepts might seem hard to grasp, but all you need to do as a convincer is to try them for one week. That's all you need to be convinced that they work. Without that commitment then there is really no point continuing reading this book.

Still here ... great! Now I want to give you some more understanding about how your mind works, so here goes. I have a rather unconventional way of explaining your conscious/unconscious mind to you, so go with it.

Your conscious mind means everything that you are aware of right now. Now I want you to start to think about how you are sitting and notice the way your arms are resting and holding this book. Now I want you to notice any sounds in the room or outside the room.

Now I want you to notice how you are breathing right now and notice your focus onto the words of this page. Notice how your head and neck are resting comfortably.

The unconscious mind is everything else that you were not aware of until I drew your attention to it. We buy products first with our unconscious mind. You only find out about it when your conscious mind catches up!

So when you are selling, who do you want to be selling to, the part of the mind that makes the decisions or the part that receives the instructions?

Did you know that 93% of all communication is non-verbal? Research shows us that 55% is physiology, 38% is tonality and 7% is words.

Okay, let's cut the boring facts and picture this instead: you are in front of your next client and you are going through your standard spiel about your product or service. He doesn't seem to be particularly interested, but instead of paying attention to what he is interested in and tailoring your pitch to fit your client's needs, you just carry on regardless! Does this sound familiar?

Why do we do this? Because we have not taken any steps to find out what he really needs or more importantly how he gets convinced to buy something.

Every time you sell something to someone, that person will convince themselves in some way based on their criteria. They do this by running certain patterns unconsciously and then bringing the results to the conscious level.

Sorry to repeat myself but this is important. *They run patterns unconsciously. They will have a specific strategy of buying.*

If you are able to pay attention to your clients' unconscious communication, then you will be able to detect their buying strategy and are much more likely to sell your product or service to them.

Are you getting excited? Thought so!

So the key is to detect your clients' unconscious buying strategy. Part of this will be their criteria and part of this will be the way they filter their world unconsciously.

I will explain what I mean by filtering shortly, but will start with criteria. Unskilled salespeople will just pitch their products totally unaware of what is important to the other person and will pitch based on what is important to them instead of their client.

Advertising companies pay millions of pounds every year for research into people's criteria so that the exact language and phrasing can be used to sell their products. The key is to link your product or service with the person's criteria. You need to find out what is important to that person and then you can genuinely influence them.

So if you find out that their criteria is speed, aesthetic looks and price, then your job is to link their criteria as being the benefits of your product or service. For example, if you are selling them a photocopier:

Salesperson: "This photocopier is twice the speed of your old one and look how good it looks. I will make sure you get a favourable price. Does this sound good?"

Criteria are like verbal triggers that evoke emotions and these can be positive or negative. You can influence a person's choice by finding out those triggers and then firing them back exactly as the other person expressed them.

Criteria = HOT BUTTONS

If you are an experienced salesperson you will already know this. As I said at the start, I am not trying to teach you how to suck eggs, honest! But let me ask you this question:

Do you actually sell to your clients' hot buttons?

You see, from my experience, most people who know about this are not using it to their advantage. If you are aware of what your clients' hot buttons are, you can hold their interest, and when the hot buttons are fired, your client will feel the emotions attached to those words. In other words you are speaking their language, literally!

Criteria are values and come from the emotional part of the brain and not the logical part; right brain rather than left brain. People buy products based on emotions not logic. Recent research into neuroscience has shown that the limbic system of the brain, the area which governs our feelings, is more powerful than the neocortex, the area that controls intellect. So the key is to work on an emotional level and understand their unconscious patterns.

People don't buy what they need ... they buy what they want

Let's go even deeper than that. If we go back to basics of the conscious/unconscious mind, you can understand the process more clearly. By the way, some books will use the words "subconscious mind". This is exactly the same as "unconscious mind".

It is important for us to understand how our behaviour manifests, so right now I want you to take a look at the following diagram. It is not as complicated as it looks! Stay with me and it will all make sense.

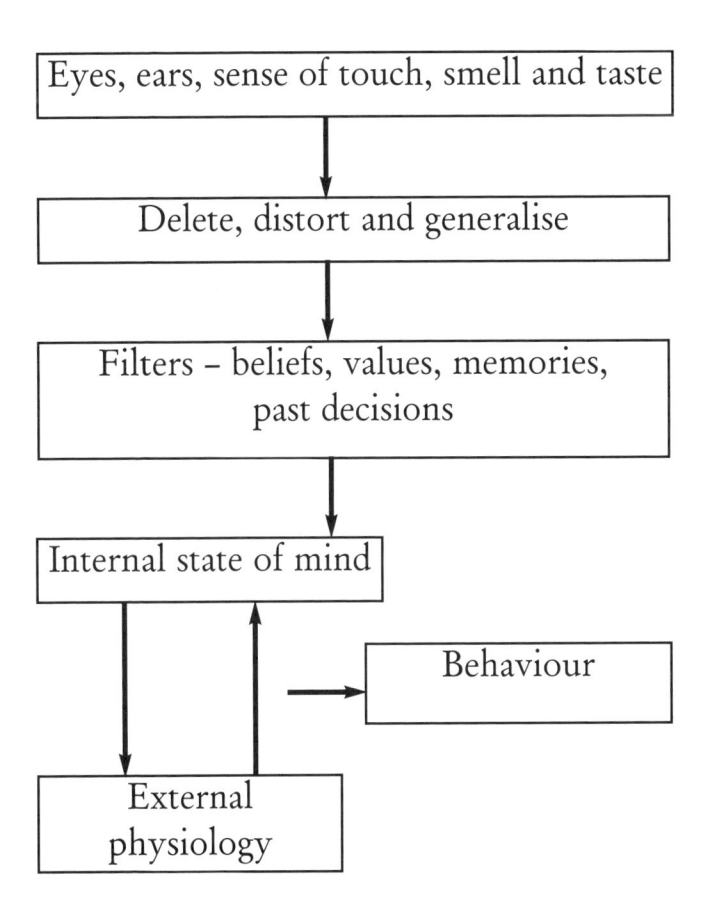

```
┌─────────────────────────────────────────────┐
│  Eyes, ears, sense of touch, smell and taste │
└─────────────────────────────────────────────┘
                      │
                      ▼
┌─────────────────────────────────────────────┐
│          Delete, distort and generalise      │
└─────────────────────────────────────────────┘
                      │
                      ▼
┌─────────────────────────────────────────────┐
│      Filters – beliefs, values, memories,    │
│                past decisions                │
└─────────────────────────────────────────────┘
                      │
                      ▼
┌──────────────────────┐
│ Internal state of mind│ ──────────▶ ┌─────────────┐
└──────────────────────┘              │  Behaviour  │
       │        ▲                     └─────────────┘
       ▼        │
┌──────────────┐
│   External   │
│  physiology  │
└──────────────┘
```

So let me explain the diagram. We all take information in through our senses: our eyes, ears, our sense of touch, smell and taste. That is 2 million bits of information per second.

Imagine you have to research something and you are given 100 different books and magazines to do this research, but you have to make some sense of it all. You would start by reading some of the books in order of importance and relevance, and then, as you were reading, you would delete the information that you consider to be irrelevant to your research.

Now think if you were asked to do that same task in a matter of just 1 second. You get the drift. It is impossible to do this in a matter of weeks, let alone seconds. This is the metaphor for 2 million bits of information per second.

Instead the brain has a way of getting rid of some information that it considers to be irrelevant and this process is called "filtering". The first part of the filtering process includes deletion, distortion and generalisation. After this has happened, the information will then go through another process to make it more manageable. It goes through a filtering process that is very much individual to each person. This will include our beliefs, values, memories and past decisions.

Now this is where it gets interesting, as once the brain has gone through all of that we then create our own internal movie of the outside world. Pretty cool, isn't it, when you think about the process? By the way, all of this happens without any conscious awareness and it happens quicker than you could blink an eye.

The internal movie that you have created will then create or alter your internal state of mind, and this in turn will change your external physiology or body language. All of this above process then creates your behaviour.

Imagine two people both going to the same destination on holiday and they are both on the same flight. One person can't wait to go and one person isn't so enthusiastic about it. Person one finds it really easy to get up at 2 o'clock in the morning as he is excited at the prospect of going to the Bahamas and he has an internal movie that would go something like this:

"I can't wait to get to the airport and have a look around the duty free. Then I love the take-off, it's so cool. I can just imagine sitting in that comfortable chair on the beach with the sun beating down on my body and the sand beneath my feet. I can't wait to do all the water sports, especially scuba."

Okay, you get the movie by now.

Now let's tackle the other person. Remember he is on the same flight and is going to the same destination. This is how he sees it:

"Oh, no, I hate airports. They are so expensive and I know it is going to be a bumpy flight and I am probably going to get airsick. I bet the hotel is going to be 2-star and I'm sure the food is going to be crap, just like the weather. And I bet I get food poisoning as well as sunstroke."

Okay, I know what you are thinking, stop exaggerating, Lawrence. Well I have met loads of people like this, and the mind movies that they play inside their heads totally affect the way that they behave. So you can see what has happened with these two people who are both going to experience the same event. Both will have a different experience based entirely on the way they construct the images in their head ahead of time.

Change the images in your head and that will then change the emotional state that you are in, which will send different messages to your brain and change the way you feel and the way that you behave. Your focus of attention will depict how you see the world.

If you were to go out and buy a new car, I guarantee that for the next few days you will see that make of car that you have just bought everywhere you look! How? The point is those cars were always there to notice, but your brain was not paying attention to them.

Your focus changes and then you start seeing things in the environment that are relative to what you are paying attention to. The same can happen in reverse. We have all done this at some point. You lose your car keys and you search all around the house to find them. You make a circuit of the house and when you can't find them you go back over the same circuit! I did six circuits once looking for my keys, only to find them in the very first place that I looked.

But why could I not see them? They were there but I could not see them. This is called a negative hallucination. Our eyes see it, but contrary to the belief that it is our eyes that see, it is actually our brain. So because our brain is not paying attention, as it is focused elsewhere, it doesn't bother letting your eyes know!

Filters = what you pay attention to

Just for a bit of fun and to prove it is not our eyes that see but our brain, try this. I want you to stare at the dot for one minute and don't take your eyes off the dot. After a minute, look up at the ceiling and keep staring until you see the image. It's worth doing...

So you see, it is our brain that sees, not our eyes.

Each of your clients will have a different internal movie when you are selling to them.

Wouldn't it be useful to know what their internal movie is and then to be able to pitch your product or service as if you are in their movie?

All the clients you deal with have a specific internal process they go through in order to make a decision. Their unconscious mind will go through a series of steps before they become convinced to buy your product. They will filter out anything that they don't think is important to them.

A bedtime story! Are you ready? Let's begin...

Imagine it is 3 am and you are in bed. You are sound asleep in a deep slumber. Suddenly you hear a thud that is so loud it wakes you up instantly. You listen again and you hear a similar noise. You start to make a mental picture of what you think it is. "Oh my God", you think, "It must be an intruder!"

From your mental picture your fight or flight response quickly kicks in. You get up and creep around the landing, picturing the worst-case scenario. Your physiology changes as the adrenaline rapidly goes off the scale!

Then you hear the noise again and realise that it is just the boiler firing up! Because the central heating pipes are old, they were rattling around amplifying the noise.

This is distortion at work because this is how you were filtering the information that was coming in through your senses. You created your own internal movie of the event.

Take a look at this picture. Say "yes" to yourself if you see trees. Say "yes" if you see grass. Say "yes" if you see a white picnic rug. Say "yes" if you see a ship.

Say "yes" if you see Napoleon.

Go to the next page if you don't see him.

The brain will look at this image and try to match it with other known images and once it finds something familiar, it deletes any other possibilities and doesn't look beyond this, instead it just generalises. This process is part of filtering.

So, like some of you with Napoleon, your clients will only pay attention to certain things. They will unconsciously filter out the information they consider irrelevant, editing and shaping what they allow to come in from the outside. In the sales arena your biggest advantage is finding out how your clients filter information. When you understand how they filter their world, you can present your product so it fits them perfectly.

So the secret of these six questions is what you do with them. In other words, by paying attention to how your clients answer each question, you will be able to determine how their minds filter information and what their minds pay attention to, and therefore you can adapt your pitch to fit the way that they filter.

When you follow these six questions, you can shorten your sales cycle, ensuring that you hit those targets and sell at a much higher level than ever before.

The key = sell to suit your clients' filters

Let's tackle the first question...

What is important to you about buying a ....?

This is a precise question. Remember, you must ask the question precisely and then extract the information you need from their answer. The key is exactly how you use that information.

When answering the first of the six questions, people will reply in one of two ways. They will either move towards what they want or away from what they don't want.

The filter is Towards v Away

Towards traits
Towards people think in terms of goals to be achieved, they move towards benefits. They are motivated, energised and excited about achieving their goals. On the downside they sometimes can't recognise a problem or what to avoid so they can be perceived as a bit naive by others.

Towards language
Towards people use specific language such as "achieve", "obtain", "gain", "benefits", "have", "attain" and "advantages". They will talk about what they want rather than what they don't want.

Towards body language
These people will do a lot of head-nodding, gestures of agreement and they will generally point towards something, whether it be finger-pointing, hand-pointing or entire body-pointing.

Away from traits
Away from people can come across as being very negative and cynical since they always think in terms of moving away from problems. Funnily

enough, they actually get truly motivated when there is a threat or deadline! They always try to avoid things that might cause them possible pain. On the upside they are really good at troubleshooting and solving problems. They often see obstacles ahead of time and pick up on what to avoid. Away from people have trouble maintaining their focus because they like to problem-solve and move onto the next problem.

Away from language
They will use language such as "avoid", "problems", "won't have to", "prevent" and "fix". They will mention stuff that they want to avoid.

Away from body language
These people normally shake their heads instead of nod in agreement. Their gestures usually suggest disagreement.

"40% of people are toward, 40% are away from. The remaining 20% are a mixture of both." *Roger Bailey*

The best way of illustrating this concept is through real conversations. I have included some actual transcripts from conversations that I have had whilst using these techniques.

I want you to read these and decide for yourself what each person's pattern is. Are they a towards person or away from person? You will find the answers on page 104 of this book.

Conversation 1
Lawrence: Hi, Do you mind if I ask you a couple of questions?
Person 1: No, not at all.
Lawrence: So what's important to you about buying a car?
Person 1: Well, I want something that looks good and leaves a good impression as this is important in my line of work.
Lawrence: What else is important?
Person 1: I want it quite sporty.
Lawrence: And why is that important?
Person 1: Because I want it to be fun and exciting to drive.

Is this person a towards or away from kind of person?

Conversation 2

Lawrence: What are you looking to implement?

Person 2: We actually need a new marketing system.

Lawrence: What's important to you about a new marketing system?

Person 2: I know that if we don't get one then the company is in big trouble as there is so much competition out there that we don't want to be left behind, and I don't want to be peddling backwards.

Lawrence: So, what else is important?

Person 2: Our old system is too expensive and it takes far too long to get any leads in.

Notice *how* people answer, not what they say. People will either move towards benefits or away from problems. Sometimes you have to probe deeper if you can't extract the information on the first question. If this happens, ask the following questions:

- Why is that important?
- What will having that do for you?
- What's in it for you?
- What's the point?

Listen carefully after the word "because" since it will always be followed by a towards or away from statement.

Putting it into practice
Once you have worked out whether someone is a towards benefits or an away from problems person, you can then tailor your pitch accordingly, literally feeding back to them their own thinking patterns. *There is nothing more powerful in communication than having your thought patterns fed right back to you.*

Selling to a towards kind of person
Person 3: I am thinking of buying a laptop computer.
Salesperson: Great, let me show you one. With this one you can achieve far superior results, and it has many advantages as you will be able to work on the move as well as at home. You can make much more use of your time and you will become more efficient. You will be able to create loads of cool stuff, including your own CDs and even DVDs.

You are doing two things here. You are linking their criteria with the benefits and you are talking their language as you are feeding back to them their unconscious thinking/buying patterns.

Selling to an away from kind of person
Person 4: I am thinking of buying a laptop computer.
Salesperson: Great, let me show you one. With this one you won't be stuck in the office anymore, restricting you and your time, and you won't have to go down to the local design shop every time you want to burn a CD or DVD. You can avoid backstrain from carrying your old computer. I've seen your old one, it is like a two-stone brick!

Selling to a mixture of both
Occasionally you will come up against those 20% of people who will be equally towards and away. The same rules apply. All you have to do is to listen to their language patterns and then feed them back to them.

That was the first question. Now onto the second question.

What are you looking for now in relation to what you had in the past?

When you ask this second question, you will get one of two responses, but remember it's how you read the response and how you use that information that counts.

Once again there are two distinct thinking patterns that come off the back of this question.

Try this:

Imagine there are three flags in front of you, the Italian flag, the Belgium flag and the Swiss flag. Now ask yourself this question:

What is the relationship between these three?

Take a moment and answer the question in your mind. Go on, really think about it!

Some people will see the flags as all being different since they are flags from different countries, but some people will see them as being the same since they are all flags.

Now imagine you are at work, and standing in front of the photocopier are two men and one woman who you have never seen around the office before. They are having a deep conversation between themselves. Now ask yourself this question: what is the relationship between these three people?

Take another moment and answer the question in your mind.

In this example, some people will see them as being part of the same group and that they are all work colleagues, they come from the same company, and some people will see them as being different; in other words, there are two men and one woman and they are all of different ages. Your response depends on how you filter your world.

The filter is Sameness v Difference

Some people will filter their world and always see things in terms of being the same and some people will filter their world and see things in terms of being different. Remember, a filter is simply how you pay attention to the world, what you focus your attention on and what you don't. Do you focus your attention on sameness or do you see differences?

Sameness traits
Sameness people like more of the same thing each time – they like to fit things into boxes and give them labels. These are the kind of people that will go into a restaurant and always order the same dish. It is important to note that sameness traits will be context-dependent.

What I mean by this is, for example, I seek sameness when it comes to food. I am so boring when it comes to food that I always order a chicken korma in an Indian restaurant, but there are differences in other areas, such as going on holiday, since I don't want to go back to the same place each year. I want something new, something different. Sameness people generally like things to stay the same, so they hate change and are likely to fight change all the way!

Sameness language
Sameness people use specific language such as "I would like the same as before", "we have a lot in common", "totally the same", "this is the same as", "this is identical", "as you already know".

Difference traits
Difference people always like to try something new. They are the kind to be adventurous when ordering food in a restaurant. These are the kind of people who love change and thrive on it, since they get bored easily.

Difference language
Difference kind of people use specific language such as "unique", "totally different to last time", "brand new", "unlike anything else", "completely different than before", "unusual".

Once again the best way of showing you this is through real conversations. Read these passages and decide for yourself what each person's pattern is. Are they a sameness or differences kind of person? You will find the answers on page 104 if you need them.

Lawrence: I hear you are interested in training some of your salesforce.
Person 5: Yes, that's right.
Lawrence: I know you have already had some form of training last year, so what are you looking for now in relation to what you had in the past?
Person 5: Well, the bottom line is I want something new and inspirational. I want it to be effective in the real world.
Lawrence: What else are you looking for in relation to what you had in the past?
Person 5: I want the training to be of value but fun, I want it to be different to last time. I want to energise the salesforce.
Lawrence: Can I ask what you had last time?

Here is another example:

Lawrence: Can I ask you about the speaker you had last year?
Person 6: Yes, sure.
Lawrence: Was he good?
Person 6: Yes he was.
Lawrence: What did you take away with you?
Person 6: He told us all about the value of teamwork and relationship building.

Lawrence: So what are you looking for now in relation to what you had in the past?
Person 6: We are looking to do the same sort of thing with you and carry on the theme.
Lawrence: How long do you want me to talk?
Person 6: About the same sort of time as last year, 45 minutes.

Notice how people answer, not what they say. People will either seek sameness or differences. So listen out for whether your potential clients are interested in uniqueness or if they want the same as before. If they seek differences then you need to sell them lots of unique selling points, and if they seek sameness, then you need to sell them more of the same, but *with added benefits.*

Putting it into practice
Once again you are powerfully feeding back to them their own thought patterns during your communication. Firstly, with regard to selling to a sameness kind of person, let's pick up the last conversation.

Lawrence: Can I ask you about the speaker you had last year?
Person 6: Yes, sure.

Lawrence: Was he good?
Person 6: Yes he was.
Lawrence: What did you take away with you?
Person 6: He told us all about the value of teamwork and relationship building.
Lawrence: So what are you looking for now in relation to what you had in the past?
Person 6: We are looking to do the same sort of thing with you and carry on the theme.
Lawrence: How long do you want me to talk?
Person 6: About the same sort of time as last year, 45 minutes.

The conversation continues...

Lawrence: I was thinking of doing a similar sort of thing to the speaker that you had last year, but I would add some other topics that will be of value to your company. Does that sound good?
Person 6: Great!

Now selling to a difference kind of person, picking up from the previous conversation:

Lawrence: I hear you are interested in training some of your salesforce.
Person 5: Yes, that's right.

Lawrence: I know you have already had some form of training last year, so what are you looking for now in relation to what you had in the past?
Person 5: Well, the bottom line is I want something new and inspirational. I want it to be effective in the real world.
Lawrence: What else are you looking for in relation to what you had in the past?
Person 5: I want the training to be of value but fun, I want it to be different to last time. I want to energise the salesforce.
Lawrence: Can I ask what you had last time?

The conversations continues…

Lawrence: I can assure you that this will be totally different to last time.
Person 5: Good.
Lawrence: Let me talk you through the unique nature of this sales training.

So as you can see in both the above examples, you have gained an understanding of what they seek, whether they seek the same as what they had last time or if they are looking for something completely different, and then you have simply given them what they seek. Once again you are speaking their unconscious language as you are feeding back to them their unconscious decision-making strategies.

Okay, on to question three...

When you make a decision, do you like to know all the details or the big picture?

This is very straightforward to explain since some people require lots and lots of detail and others hate it and just want an overview. It's important to know which one the client requires if you are to give them what they need.

If you give out a lot of detail to a person who filters the overview, they will just get bored and switch off, as they just want the big picture. On the other hand, if you give just an overview of information to someone who needs specific details, then you won't keep their attention or convince them to buy your product.

The filter is Details v Overview

Remember the filter is simply what you pay attention to. Do you focus your attention on the specific details or on the big picture?

Detail traits
Detail people are the type of people who notice what you are wearing, and they can walk into a house and notice instantly if you have changed something. A detail person will notice the birds, the palm trees, the texture of the sand and the colour of the sky, rather than just the beach. They like to create steps and sequences to achieve something. They make great accountants with all that attention to detail!

Detail language
Detail people use language such as "can I have the details?", "I would to know exactly what you mean", "can you tell me specifically?", "what precisely do you mean?"

Overview traits
Overview people will simply notice the beach and not the finer detail that is in front of them. They love to give out summaries and overviews, rather than getting into the specific details.

Overview language
Overview people use specific language such as "let me summarise for you", "if we look at the big picture", "in general", "let me give you an overview".

Here is a reconstructed conversation for you to see the differences. Read it and decide for yourself what each person's pattern is. Who is the detail person and who is the overview one? You will find the answers on page 104, as if you need them now!

The adoring couple!
Male: Honey, I'm home
Female: Hi dear, how was your day?
Male: You know, the same as usual.
Female: So what did you do today?
Male: I sold some houses.
Female: Tell me more.
Male: I sold three houses today.
Female: Where were the houses? Were they two-, three-, four- or five-bedroom houses? How long had they been on the market? How many people were after them? Were they in good condition?
Male: Look, I can't be bothered to talk about it

now. I've had a hard day at the office and it isn't any different from last time I sold three houses!
Female: Okay, I'm only interested in your day. You don't have to bite my head off!

Can you relate to this?

This relationship is a classic example of how two people with different needs can end up. One person needs a lot of detail and the other needs just an overview. So the person that needs the detail thinks the other is not interested, but this is not the case. The other person who just needs an overview thinks, "Why are you asking me all these bloody questions? Would you just shut up!" There is a total mismatch of communication between the couple.

This can also happen in the sales arena where you can easily lose clients if you are not aware of their needs. Notice how people answer, not what they say. People will either seek simply an overview or they will need the specific details, so listen out for what your clients need.

It is therefore imperative to find out your clients' needs before you begin to sell to them. One simple question and you can avoid losing a customer. If your customer filters overview, then just give him an overview. If he needs lots of details, go through the details with him until he is fully satisfied, but find out what he needs first.

The next two precision questions are part of what is known as the *convincing process*. They are asked in accordance with one another and are vital in the sales arena.

As you know, most clients will not even consider spending their money until they are fully convinced of your product or service. Therefore, one of the most important things in sales is to know how a client gets convinced. To detect what is known as their convincer channel, you must ask them two questions.

How do you know a product is worth buying?

People will answer this question in one of four ways, depending on which sensory channel they gather information through. But, how do you find out what sensory channel they are in?

Remember the diagram on page 21 explaining how our behaviour is created. It showed us how we first take information in through our senses. Visually through our eyes, hearing through our ears, and feeling through our sense of touch, smell and taste. This is how we gather our information and these are our sensory channels.

Now if we translate that to this example, then people either have to:

• SEE some evidence to be convinced
• HEAR someone or something to be convinced
• READ something, for example reports or testimonials, to be convinced

Or

• TRY something to be convinced, like trying on new clothes, sitting behind the wheel of a car or testing out the keyboard on a new computer.

The filter is the Convincer Channel

Here are some more conversations, and I want you to try to work out what sensory channel each person gets convinced in. Answers on page 104 as usual!

These are taken from real conversations, but I have summarised them for our purposes.

First conversation
Lawrence: How do you know a product is worth buying?
Person 7: I would have to see it before I buy.

Second Conversation
Lawrence: How do you know a product is worth buying?
Person 8: Well, I'm the sort that needs to try it a few times before I would actually buy it.

Third conversation
Lawrence: How do you know a product is worth buying?
Person 9: What do you mean by that?
Lawrence: How do you normally decide on a product?
Person 9: I don't buy anything unless I have heard about it from someone else.

Fourth conversation
Lawrence: How do you know a product is worth buying?
Person 10: I normally read those *Which* reports. They're very good, you know.

Fifth conversation
Lawrence: How do you know a product is worth buying?
Person 11: I would have to be shown the product a few times.
Lawrence: What do you mean?
Person 11: Well, I normally see it in a few catalogues like Argos and Littlewoods first, and then I would take a look in the shops and see if I like it, but I would probably buy from a catalogue as the prices are normally cheaper.

Sixth conversation
Lawrence: How do you know a product is worth buying?
Person 12: It all depends on how much it costs.
Lawrence: But if it was the right price for you, how do you know it is worth buying?
Person 12: I normally then ask someone's advice.
Lawrence: Whose advice would you seek?

Person 12: The shop assistant if I trust them. If not, I would just ask around before I buy it.

Imagine you are listening intently and are totally focused on what your client is about to say but for some reason you don't hear what sensory system they are in and you miss it completely, what do you do?

First of all, DON'T PANIC!!

Really don't worry...there is another way. This is where it really gets interesting.

Our eyes give a clue as to the way we think as we snatch information from different parts of our brain, similar to a filing cabinet. Our eyes will indicate what sensory system we are in at any given time. All you have to do is know what to look for.

Intrigued? Follow me to the diagrams.

So imagine that you are looking at someone face on. Notice where the eyes are positioned right now. Take a mental picture of that, and then move on to the next page.

Now take a look at this diagram. When we are in the visual sensory system, we will either look up to our left or right. In this instance he is specifically looking up to our right as we view him. This happens when we are visually remembering stored images.

When we look up to the other direction we are still visualising, but we are constructing images instead.

A nugget of interest!
An interesting point to note here is that people who spell very well will always look up

to the right (as we view them) to the visually remembered stored images side, so they will see the correct version of the word each time they go to spell it; however, people who spell very badly will generally look up to the left (as we view them) and because they do this they are having to construct the word from scratch each time, and therefore because they are not grabbing the information from a remembered source, they normally get the word wrong each time.

Sorry to interrupt the proceedings, but I find that so fascinating.

Notice now that the eyes are in the midway position but they are to the left as you are looking at someone. This is when we are in the hearing sensory system, but because the eyes are over to the left, this means that we are constructing sounds in our brain.

Notice now that the eyes are in the midway position but they are to the right as you are looking at them. This is when we are in the hearing sensory system, but more specifically when we are remembering stored sounds in our brain.

Now notice how the eyes have gone all the way down to the left as we view them. This is when we are in the feeling sensory system, when we are connecting with our feelings and emotions. This is called the kinesthetic system.

Notice now how the eyes have gone all the way down but to the other side. This is when we are listening to our internal voice or dialogue, or our "self-talk".

Now some people they might find this difficult to imagine because they have never noticed this before, but I want you to get a buzz out of this, so what I really want you to do is this:

Over the next five conversations that you have, I want you to just notice where that person's eyes go as you communicate with them. I guarantee once you have done that you will be blown away!

The strange thing is, this was always there to notice, but it was just a matter of tuning in.

"So am I blind?", I hear you say. No, the good news is that you most certainly are not. Once again this was about how you set your filters, your brain's focus, what your brain decided to pay attention to. If your brain was not set to look, then you would naturally miss it completely.

Let's take it a step further still. This will also help in understanding what kind of language patterns you need to feed back to each client. The way we access information then gets transferred to our speech patterns. So if you are accessing in the visual sensory system, then you will use a visual language pattern to communicate. For example, "I see what you mean" or "I can picture this clearly now".

If you are accessing in the hearing sensory system, then you will use a hearing language pattern. For example, "I hear what you are saying" or "that sounds good".

In the feeling or kinesthetic sensory system, you will use a feeling language pattern. For example, "I feel that you are right" or "I want to touch base with you".

Take a look at some typical visual, hearing and feeling words:

Visual
- See • Focus • Clear • Bright • Hazy
- Colour • Dim • Look • View • Foggy
- Gaze • Glow • Appear • Envisage
- Outlook • Foresee • Watch • Imagine
- Visible • Clarify

Hearing
- Listen • Hear • Tune • Voice • Cry
- Rings a bell • Chatter • Discuss • Whine
- Silence • Call • Mention • Resounding
- Sound • Tell • Loud • Snap • Volume
- Talk • Say • Click

Feeling
- Touch • Feel • Grasp • Handle • Pressure
- Cling • Numb • Soft • Tremble • Rough
- Warm • Shiver • Shake • Hold • Relaxed
- Absorb • Impact • Smell • Tense • Whiff

KEY EXPRESSIONS

Visual
I get a clear picture of that
The outlook is bleak
Things are looking up
I can see how it works

Hearing
I'm glad to hear it
We're in tune with each other
Listen to yourself
That rings a bell

Feeling
A taste of fear
Get in touch with reality
I can't grasp that
I feel that you're right
Warm regards

So now let's just recap.

• The point is to find out what sensory system your client is making his decision in.

• You can do this by either listening to his language patterns or watching his eyes.

• The final step is to learn how and what to feed back to him.

Putting it into practice
So once you have worked out which of the four sensory channels your client uses to make his decision, you simply pitch back your product using his sensory language. In this way you can convince him of your product or service.

So if your clients' sensory channel is *SEE*, feed them back visual words such as "I would like to *show* you a sample" or "I think you should *see* one".

You could also paint them a mental picture since they are in a visual sensory system at this point and this is where the information will best hit as you will be communicating with them in their unconscious communication system.

If their sensory channel is *HEAR*, feed them back hearing words such as "That *sounds* all right, doesn't it?" or "Is there anything else you need to *hear* or *discuss*?"

If their channel is *TRY*– this is the feeling sensory channel – feed them back feeling words such as "You'll want to *try* it out, won't you?" or "Get a *feel* for how this works".

If there is a product available and it is possible, then place the product in their hands, let them play with it. Get them behind the wheel of the car or get them to try the article on for size. If there is no available product or you are selling a service, then instead get them to connect with their feelings in some way. Remember these are internal *feeling* people.

If their channel is *READ*, make sure you have lots of testimonials for them to read, or reports or articles on the benefits of the product.

If you can't notice their sensory system in their language patterns, then look out for when their eyes go down to the right as you view them – see page 77 – since then they are listening to their internal voice. We do this when we read. Most people will read the words out inside their heads as they go along.

The second stage of the convincing process is known as the convincer cycle. Before people are convinced of buying something, they will need to go through their own convincer cycle. To detect this, ask them the next question.

How many times would you need to (see) (hear) (read) (try) to be convinced that the product is for you?

- Just once

- A set number of times

- A period of time

- Always changing

Let me explain this. Some people will be able to make instant decisions and therefore they will cycle through their convincer cycle just once.

Some people will cycle through a set number of times, maybe two or three, before they get truly convinced.

Some people will only get convinced over a period of time, and that time has to elapse before they will be ready to buy.

Some people will always be changing their mind and go through a continuous cycle.

The filter is the Convincer Cycle

It is interesting to note that the majority of the population will cycle through two or three times before they get convinced to buy something. Advertisers have picked up on this phenomenon, and by watching particular adverts, especially in the States, then you will have seen the rule of three being applied.

I will give you an example of a typical advert using these principles.

It's now time to go to a commercial break! Imagine a cheesy voice-over actor...

'So if you buy this new veggie-peeler pro, then we will throw in a free refill for your veggie-peeler pro." *Convincer number 1*

"But wait, don't buy just yet, because if you buy today, then we will also throw in set of fabulous carving knives." *Convincer number 2*

"But that's not all, because if you pick up the phone and call us within the next hour, then we will also include a free cookbook with over 100 tantalising recipes." *Convincer number 3* "So pick up that phone now!"

Welcome back from the commercial break. Are you convinced to buy the veggie-peeler pro? This product doesn't actually exist, but it sounds quite good, doesn't it!

Sorry, I've been spending too long on my own writing this book – I must get out more!

Okay, let's get back on track. So whatever your buyer answered from the previous precision question with regards to his sensory channel, take that and add it to the next precision question.

For example, with the first question you managed to find out that his sensory channel is read. If he needs to read about the product to be convinced to buy it, then simply tag on the next question and say, "How many times would you need to read about this product to be convinced that it is for you?" or "How many articles would you need to read to be convinced that it is for you?"

If he needs to see a product to be convinced to buy it, then simply tag on a further question and say, "How many times would you need to see this product to be convinced that it is for you?"

If he needs to hear about the product to be convinced to buy it, then simply tag on, "How many times would you need to hear about this product to be convinced that it is for you?"

If he needs to try a product to be convinced to buy it, then simply tag on, "How many times would you need to try this product out to be convinced that it is for you?"

PUTTING IT INTO PRACTICE

Just once
If you are trying to convince a person and you know they cycle through just once, then great if they say "yes". Nice and easy for you!

But if they say "no" automatically, don't waste your time, move on. Do not bother going back to them. They very rarely change their minds.

Always changing
Always changing people are the worst people to deal with, as you will need to re-establish your credibility every time you meet them. They may want to buy your product or service one day and then change their minds the next day and then change it back the following day!

Don't you just hate these people! Your best option is to get them to go inside themselves and get them to process this statement: "Only you will know when this is right for you".

Set number of times
With a set number of times people, all you have to do with them is remember what sensory

channel they get convinced in and repeat it that number of times.

If you know their convincer cycle is three, then you can use language like, "If you were to see three other examples, would you be totally convinced?"

Or better still, just show them three other examples. If you have a catalogue with a photo of the product in, then that will count as they are visually seeing the product.

The other way of doing this is to get them to imagine three different scenarios. If they are using their imagination, then they will enter into the visual sensory system, and by getting them to picture three different scenarios, then you are catering for their convincer cycle.

For example, imagine I am selling you a telecommunication system.

1. "It's a great-looking system. Just imagine the convenience of this as you can simply patch through to any work colleague on any floor. How easy is that?"

If they are an away from person, you can alter it to "No more running up those stairs to get your colleagues to answer the phone!"

2. "I was talking to one of my other clients about this system and he said that he saw this system in action at an exhibition in Germany, where they demonstrated it with over 50 companies all linked up to this one system, and the speed of it was like a bullet coming out of a gun. He said it was the best on the market and the best one he had seen at the exhibition."

3. "Also, if you do decide to buy this system, then you will be able to do a whole lot more. For example…"

Do you get the picture?

Paint them pictures!

Period of time
Period of time people will only get convinced to buy when a certain amount of time has elapsed. It will normally be a set period of time, like a couple of months. In this case you can either wait for a couple of months before you phone

them again or you can be clever with your language, phone them a few weeks later and say "I have been so busy with work, it feels like a couple of months have gone by! How did you want to proceed?"

"Nice and subtle", I hear you say!

Okay, onto the last question.

Do you like to plan things or keep them open-ended?

This is about the easiest concept to grasp.
As you can tell, this question will elicit one of two types of response. Some people will love procedure and like to plan things and some people just like to keep their options open.

The filter is Procedure v Options

Procedure people
These are people who like to plan things and they are highly sequenced and organised. They just love lists! They are the type who would rather follow a map than try to find the destination by luck. They like to always have some sort of procedure with a beginning and an end to complete a task. For these people, life and death depends on whether they finish the sequence that they start!

They like to be shown what to do. Even with a simple task like dancing, they would rather take some lessons so they can follow a procedure and feel they know what they are doing. This way they feel confident when they get on the dance floor.

When selling to these kind of people, they need to be sold to in stages, in a sequence, and must have some form of closure.

Option people
On the other side of the coin, option people like to keep things open-ended. Rather than closure, they require flexibility. They are known as option people because, as you might expect, they

like to keep their options open. They love to think in terms of unlimited options and unlimited possibilities. These people hate following the rules since they hate procedure. They like to find their own way of doing things. If you give them a task, the chances are they will change the task in some way to suit them.

Some people will know exactly what they are doing on the weekends, but option people would prefer to just play it by ear. You never know, something better might come up.

Selling to procedure people
Procedure people like closure. They want to know when a sequence will end. Use language such as "I can take you through this step by step", "let me show you how this works", "let me explain the procedure".

You can also simply create steps for them like this: "firstly I will show you ... secondly I must tell you about ... and thirdly let's discuss the ..."

Selling to option people
Option people don't like closure and prefer to keep their options open. Use language such as

"I can give you some good options and you can decide later" or "there are lots of choices for you, let me show you an alternative" or "the sky's the limit". Remember to give them options and not to try to close them.

Finally, with this question rather than asking them "do you like to plan things or keep things open-ended?", there is another option. Try saying, "there are four things you need to know about this product". Tell them only three things, and if they ask what the fourth is, you will know they are a sequenced or procedure person. If they don't ask, you'll know that they are not. You'll find that if they are a procedure person, they just can't help themselves as they have to know what is at the end of a sequence.

So the precision question will extract the filter, in other words do they require some form of procedure and plan or do they prefer to just keep their options open. Once you have discovered what they need, then all you have to do is give them what they want.

If you try to close an option person, then it is most likely that you will lose them. It is much better to give them space and let them feel they are making the decision.

If you give lots of options to a procedure person and you have not mapped out any kind of steps for what you are doing, it is likely that you will lose them since they need some form of closure.

If you learn to identify these patterns, then you can avoid losing a client and sell much more powerfully to each client.

SUMMARY

I thought I would conclude with a few answers to some of the questions that you might have on your mind.

I am not a mindreader, but here goes!

Firstly it does not matter if you miss the answers to one or two of the questions since any one of these questions will help you communicate your pitch in a more powerful way. Any one of these questions will help you communicate at a deeper lever than you were communicating before.

At first these patterns might seem hard to spot, but when you hear them a lot you will be amazed how obvious each pattern is to recognise. It is just a matter of tuning in and paying attention to different aspects of the conversation than you would normally.

Concentration is really the key when listening out for these patterns. Normally we would miss this kind of information in our everyday communication. Now you know what to look out for, it is easy as long as you concentrate.

When answering these questions, people can sometimes go off on a tangent. If people do go off on a tangent, then don't worry. As long as you know what you are looking for within the content, then all you need to do is pull them back to the direction you want to go down. Simply re-focus them back on track.

You can always ask the same question two or three times. You will be amazed how people love to talk about themselves!

I am often asked whether people twig what you are doing when you ask them these six questions. The honest answer is that people never pick up on it so don't get paranoid when asking them!

If you are with a person who is buying either products or services for their company and not for themselves, will the same thinking patterns apply?

This is an interesting point, but please note that most people will still buy with themselves in mind, so even if they buy on behalf of their company, you are still selling to their personal filters.

So that's about it, six simple innocent questions and you can extract all the information that you need. Weave them into a casual conversation, listen to how your clients respond and you will soon be tapping into their unconscious buying patterns, and if you do this you will be communicating at a much deeper level since you will have a map of how your clients think. Once you know how they think, you can present your product so it fits like a glove.

I really hope you have enjoyed the book and have found it of value. If you have, then please look on my website (see page 119) for further products you might want to purchase, and if you haven't, then please look on my website for further products you might want to purchase!!

Thanks again and goodbye for now

Lawrence Peyton

ANSWERS

Conversations

Person 1 = a towards person

Person 2 = an away from person

Person 5 = a differences kind of person

Person 6 = a sameness kind of person

The adoring couple

The female = detail

The male = overview

Person 7 = visual

Person 8 = try (kinesthetic)

Person 9 = hear

Person 10 = read

Person 11 = visual

Person 12 = hear

THE SIX QUESTIONS

1. What is important to you about buying a .... ?

2. What are you looking for now in relation to what you had in the past?

3. When you make a decision, do you like to know all the details or the big picture?

4. How do you know a product is worth buying?

5. How many times would you need to (see) (hear) (read) (try) to be convinced that the product is for you?

6) Do you like to plan things or keep them open-ended?

THE SIX FILTERS

Towards v Away

Sameness v Differences

Details v Overview

Convincer Channel

Convincer Cycle

Procedure v Options

NOTES

What is important to you about buying a ....?

NOTES

What are you looking for now in relation to what you had in the past?

NOTES

When you make a decision, do you like to know all the details or the big picture?

NOTES

How do you know a product is worth buying?

NOTES

How many times would you need to (see) (hear) (read) (try) to be convinced that the product is for you?

NOTES

Do you like to plan things or keep them open-ended?

TRAINING

Lawrence Leyton's company provides a wide range of consultancy, training, coaching and facilitation for solving business problems and improving business processes. Lawrence personally travels the globe talking to some of the world's biggest companies on a wide range of different subjects. We thought it would be interesting to include a brief summary of them.

Keynote speeches and seminars:

The Psychology of Success is all about giving you tools to master your emotional state and covers the characteristics of world-class performers.

What makes the difference between good and outstanding? Think about successful sports people. At this level, one tenth of a second will make all the difference in the 100 metres, one extra point will make all the difference at Wimbledon and 2mm can make all the difference at the Olympics. It can be the difference between winning a gold medal or going home with just a memory. Is that 2mm down to skill? No, it is mostly down to attitude.

You can learn how to influence your own behaviour and how to achieve a peak state of mind and maintain it. You can learn how to change a negative state into a positive one and how to change a limiting belief into an absolute certainty that you can achieve something.

High Impact Communication covers advanced communication techniques, since today more and more organisations view soft skills as essential weapons to gain real competitive advantage. Did you know that most business decisions are made on the basis of rapport rather than technical merit?

Effective communication hinges on the amount of rapport you have with the other person, whether you are communicating changes with your staff or simply making your clients feel more comfortable or dealing with that difficult customer. It is possible to learn a technique to gain rapport when it is not naturally occurring, thus giving you the competitive advantage.

Innovation in Business covers idea generation techniques, problem solving and the most effective way to achieve a creative mindstate.

Most companies, when they innovate, tend to do it only once and rely on that innovation for years! The key is to keep on innovating. You can learn how to use both creative (right brain) and analytical (left brain) skills in solving a problem and generating your ideas.

If you would like to know more about training in the six most powerful questions or any of the other topics mentioned, or if you would like to contact Lawrence Leyton International, see the website:

www.lawrenceleyton.com

ACKNOWLEDGMENTS

I would like to personally thank Lisa Minsky who has not only beautifully edited this book, but has also been a great friend to me.

I would also like to thank Jane Davidson for the wonderful jacket design.

I would like to thank Keith Kay, at Bright Interval Books, for his kind permission to use the Mona Lisa and Napoleon artwork.